Vivir la Muerte

Bastienne Schmidt
Vivir la Muerte

Living with Death in Latin America

Edited by Hans-Georg Pospischil
Texts by Karl Steinorth, Edward J. Sullivan
and Bastienne Schmidt

EDITION STEMMLE

To my father, Gerhard Schmidt

But the Gods created
For all incurable suffering,
Friend, a remedy:
Patience, to bear them
And strength.

Archilochos

Contents

Todos Santos, Guatemala, **1993**

Patzcuaro, Mexico, **1992**

Todos Santos, Guatemala, **1993**

Foreword

Karl Steinorth

Bastienne Schmidt's photographs deal with death. In many of them we are confronted with violent death in an environment that grows more brutal every day. Others document Latin American death rituals. In her own words, it was the death of her father that showed her "the need to develop a view of things in which death also has its place."

This personal need to come to terms with death motivated her to undertake a project lasting several years and devoted to a photographic documentation of the way in which people deal with death in our world. She chose Latin America as her setting. Aside from her general interest in Central and South America, she was influenced in her choice by the realization that the countries of this continent have one thing in common: a much closer and more intense involvement with death than is the case in Europe, for instance. Her own personal involvement creates a bond between Bastienne Schmidt and the victims and mourners. Thus her photos are not those of a voyeur.

Bastienne Schmidt's choice of motifs, the segment of reality she selects, the pictorial composition that she recognizes instantly – all contribute to the impression that, despite the unpleasant aspects of her subject, her pictures are right, in a formal sense, if not in fact beautiful. This may well be explained by the fact that she studied painting before turning to photography. Today, Bastienne Schmidt is a successful photojournalist, whose photos skillfully support explorations of a variety of subjects. She cites the American photographer Mary Ellen Mark as a model in the field of pictorial journalism. As she recently stated in an interview, however, she would prefer not to be seen as a photojournalist. Her wish is surely to be understood in the sense that her primary focus is upon projects she has conceived herself, such as the one which has led to publication of this book. Unlike commissioned works, the long-term projects now becoming increasingly popular among photographers are characterized by much more intense personal, often emotionally based, objectives and a deeper involvement with their chosen subjects on the part of the artists. The best of these photographic projects – as Wilfried Wiegand recently commented – are on a par with the genre of the essay on sociology or cultural history.

Aside from her documentation of a variety of death rituals practiced in Latin America, Bastienne Schmidt's photos taken in Bogota are worthy of particular mention. What interests the photographer here is the way in which people react in their families to the almost daily occurrence of murder and to the changes it causes. Some of her photographs from Bogota – so it appears to me, at least – communicate a mood, but reveal little about the underlying facts. In my opinion, it is these pictures in particular that demonstrate the power of this photographer's art to capture the viewer's gaze and force him to contemplate what he sees.

A personal remark in closing: I saw many of the photographs that appear in this volume for the first time as a member of the jury for the German Photo Award. The pictures fascinated me immediately, because they compel us to deal with the taboo subject of death. The jury's decision that this project was worthy of support through the award of a grant was reached quickly and unanimously.

To see Bastienne Schmidt's excellent photographs published in book form, complemented there by others she took in Brazil, Cuba and other Latin American countries, is a source of great joy to both the members of the jury and the awarding institution, as it shows that in this case the award has made continued work on a significant photographic project possible.

Transforming Sensibilities:
The Photography of Bastienne Schmidt

Edward J. Sullivan

The art of photography, more than any other form of aesthetic expression, has been able to evoke the most intimate of human emotions. No other method of visualization can capture, with the instant shock of recognition that we all often experience while looking at a particularly successful photographic image, the inner core of human acceptance. In her often-shocking, always striking and inevitably beautiful photographs, Bastienne Schmidt has demonstrated her power to create dramatic simulacra of the reality of all of our lives, allowing the viewer a glimpse into his or her own soul as well as into many of the areas of our imagination which we often attempt, with such vigor and force, to keep hidden from our consciousness and that of everyone around us. It makes little difference that the vast majority of Schmidt's recent work depicts scenes of a specifically Latin American reality. Although her photographs are set in Colombia, Guatemala, Mexico or other Latin nations which have experienced particularly disturbing social and political turmoil over the last decades, we are able to recognize in the participants in the often bizarre-seeming tragic dramas she records, aspects of our own imagination and our own intense preoccupation with themes of suffering and death and its consequences for those around us.

The work of Bastienne Schmidt must be considered, on one hand, as representative of a specifically late-twentieth century world situation in which the horrors of drug addiction and its consequent social conflicts, political and factional disputes over ideology, territory or material possessions or, especially, the degradation of poverty, have wrecked havoc over the psychological landscape of the "modern" consciousness. Certainly, in one or two-hundred year's time, her work will be regarded as representing the painful atmosphere as well as many of the specific disturbing events surrounding the final years of the millennium. Nonetheless, to consider her photographic art as completely rooted in the traumatic materiality of the 1990s would reduce, I believe, our comprehension of her contribution to merely temporal dimensions. Within the development of the art of photography we might attempt to establish a place for Schmidt's images along historical lines. Although her art is quintessentially of the moment in which she is working, her photographic images may also be seen within the parameters of the urge, always present in the western aesthetic imagination, to memorialize both the grandiose and the conventionally "significant" moments of human existence as well as those instants of seemingly inconsequential human behavior.

Death, pain and suffering have been the subjects of artist's concerns for centuries, yet with the invention of photography in the 1830s, the element of poignancy and the immediate impact of such themes came much more dramatically to the fore. In the 1850s the American photographers Albert Sands Sandworth and Josiah Johnson Hawes began to photograph autopsies. Although the anatomy lesson had been the subject of paintings by such distinguished artists as Rembrandt himself as well as the American Thomas Eakins, there was something much more shocking about these photographs taken in ca. 1855. Pictures such as these, as well as other nineteenth century photographic images as the thousands of portraits of deceased children (a tradition which received special attention in Mexico and other parts of Latin America, where the "cult of death" is taken as a natural part of human existence – a fact innately understood and shared by Bastienne Schmidt), provoked the morbid, voyeuristic urges as well as the pure fascination of the viewer.

The development of the transportable camera also made possible the first-hand recording of the events of human suffering associated with warfare. In the nineteenth century, such cataclysms as the terrible ferocity of the American Civil War, the Crimean War and others were registered with the objectifying force of the camera's lens. In the twentieth century, war documentary photography became the standard form of recording not only the heroics of battle but the terrible consequences for ordinary citizens. The photojournalism and war reportage of such masters as Robert Capa, Chim and others may be viewed as highly relevant to any discussion of the accomplishments of Bastienne Schmidt. Schmidt's art also realizes an inevitable kinship with other forms of twentieth century photography. The compelling and often repulsive images of Weegee (Arthur Fellig), photojournalist who specialized in record-ing images of murderers for the more sensationalistic newspapers of New York City, shares a sensibility with the immediacy and shocking quality of Schmidt's work. In addition, Schmidt's straightforward rendering of the most debased forms of human suffering also shares something of the sensibility of certain contemporary photographers whose attentions have turned to the suffering of such quintessentially late twentieth century maladies as AIDS. Rosalind Solomon, to name only one of many photographic recorders of this devastating disease, presents its effects with straightforward directness, shying away from none of the painful elements, yet not dwelling in a morbid way on any one of the many excruciating symp-toms. Bastienne Schmidt shares this sort of objectivity in the face of pain.

Viewing Bastienne Schmidt's recent exhibition (fall, 1995) at the International Center of Photography in New York, the visitor was compelled not only by the images them-selves (many of which are published in the present volume), but also by the reactions of the other viewers. Repulsion was one of the inevitable initial responses, yet what was more inter-esting to watch was the transformation of repulsion to compassion, fascination and some sort of innate understanding of the underlying reasons for and consequences of the scenes of an-guish and death that this photographer has captured. Schmidt has a unique ability to enter in-to the deepest recesses of our imaginations and to take over, if only for the brief time of viewing her art, some highly intimate corner of our response systems. Yet, the drama and the impact of these photographs is not dissipated when we leave the exhibition, close the book or put away the photograph. The pictures with which she presents us bequeath an indelible mark on our sensibilities. We are, in a way, deeply scarred, branded and altered by the experience of seeing her work. After the shock wears away, we are left with the after-image of an insight into human behavior and human reactions to extreme situations that we had never before had. Schmidt thus transforms us. Even if we do not immediately recognize this, we are, in some tiny way, not the same as we were before witnessing her art.

First Encounter with Death

Patzcuaro, Mexico, **1992**

Puno, Peru, **1990**

Puno, Peru, **1992**

Havana, Cuba, **1994**

Bogota, Colombia, **1991**

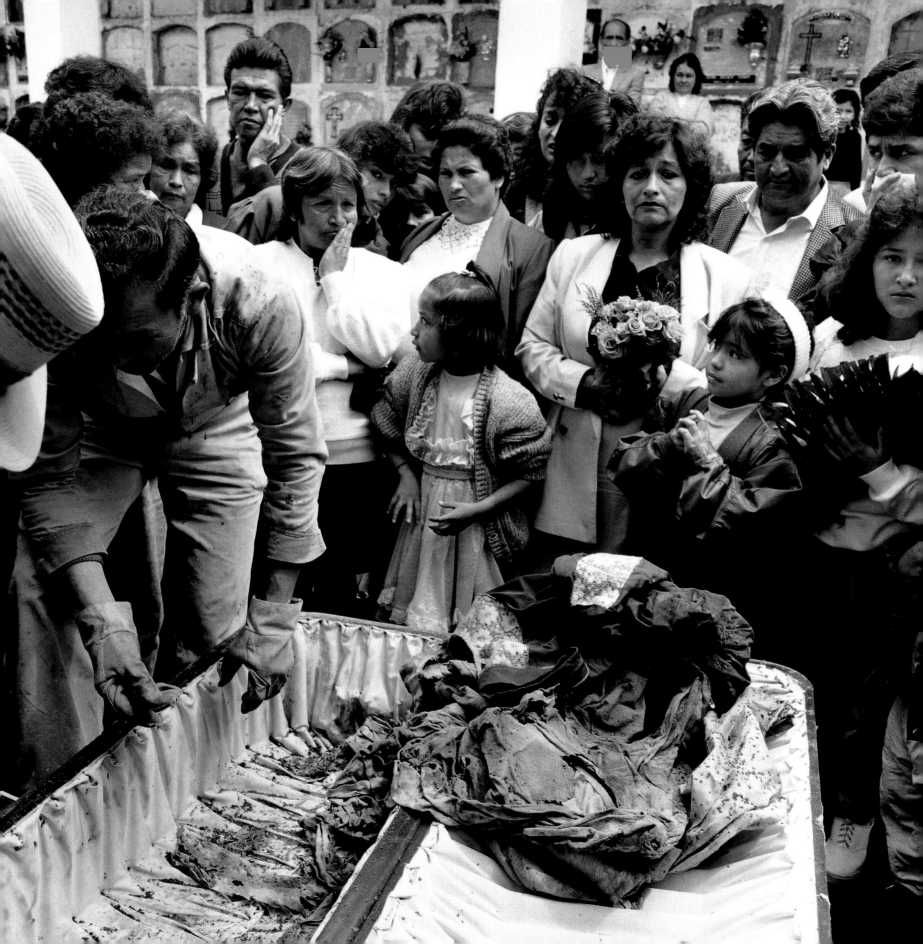

Bogota, Colombia, **1991**

Patzcuaro, Mexico, **1992**

Patzcuaro, Mexico, **1992**

Patzcuaro, Mexico, **1992**

Patzcuaro, Mexico, **1992**

Patzcuaro, Mexico, **1992**

Bogota, Colombia, **1991**

San Juan, Guatemala, **1993**

Gestures of Grief

Guajira, Colombia, **1991**

Bogota, Colombia, **1991**

Bogota, Colombia, **1991**

Cartagena, Colombia, **1991**

Zunil, Guatemala, **1993**

Zunil, Guatemala, **1993**

Puno, Peru, **1990**

Salvador, Brazil, **1994**

Bogota, Colombia, **1991**

Lima, Peru, **1990**

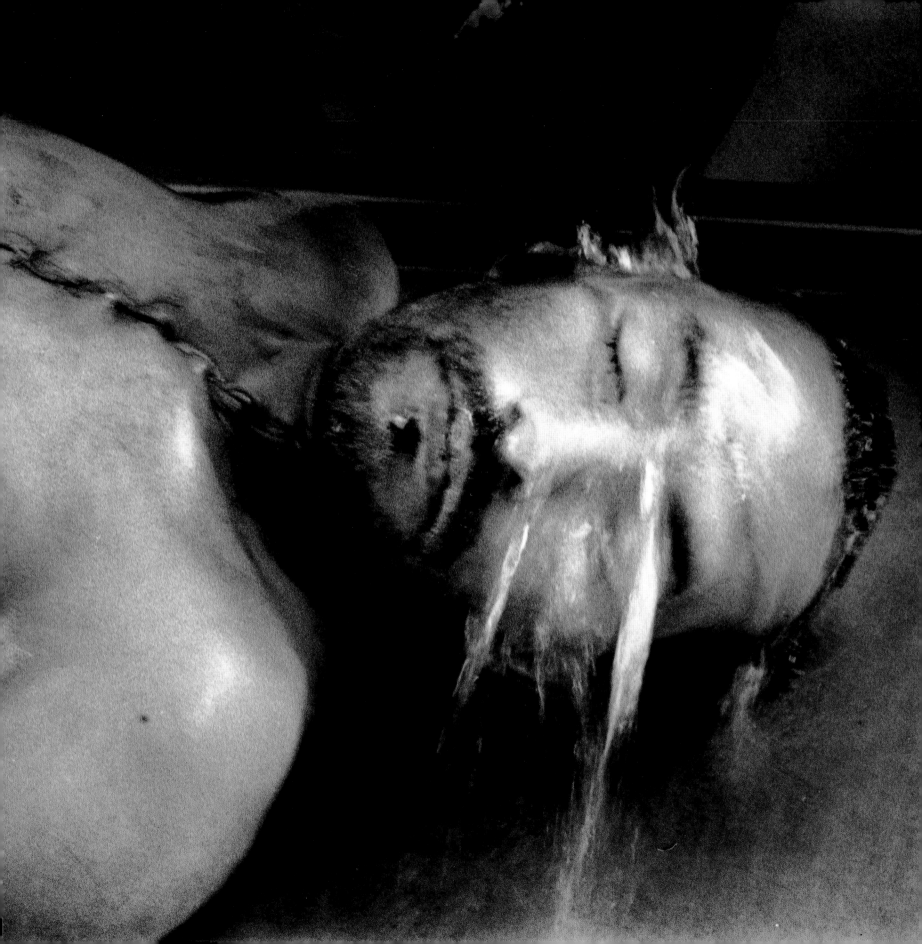

Salvador, Brazil, **1994**

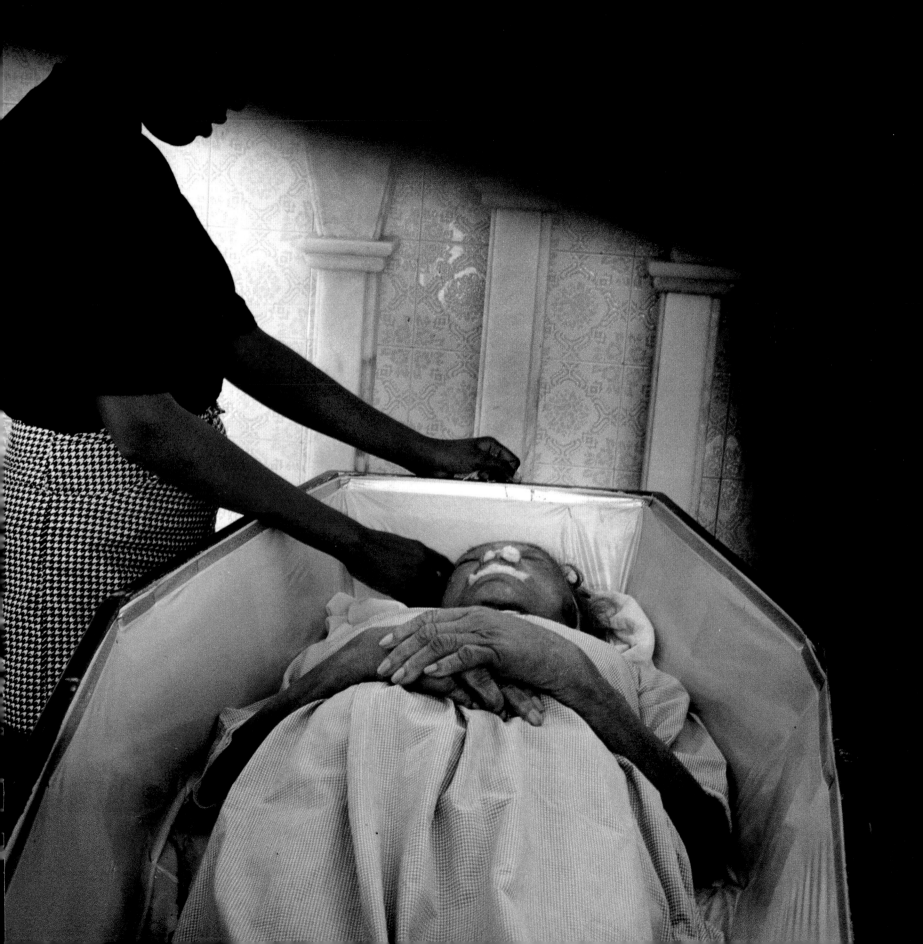

Bogota, Colombia, **1991**

Zunil, Guatemala, **1993**

Colima, Peru, **1992**

Colima, Peru, **1992**

Colima, Peru, **1992**

Salvador, Brazil, **1994**

Puno, Peru, **1992**

The Day of the Dead

Guajira, Colombia, **1991**

ARIS
DAVID
GUERRA
PERALTA

ADRIANO
BUENO. F.
Q.E.P.D.

MURIO 5
7 1984

Donatila Asis
Vda de Gutierrez

Nacio 25 marzo
1890

Murio 5 de
Febrero 1982.

Q. E.P.D.

DARTO
ATENCIO
MURIO
NOVIEM
BRE/28/83

56
ALCIDES
RAFAEL
NIVES
NUNES
MURIO

OCT 10-1984
OCT 7-1986

EN TU BREVE PASO
POR LA VIDA DEJAS
TE EN NUESTROS
CORAZONES LA
GRACIA DE TU SON
RISA Y UN RECUER
DO IMPERECEDER

Faizully G.
Campo
Carrillo

NDR
ARE

ALBERTO
CALDERON
SEPTIEMBRE
14-1988

JUAN
JESUS

68

TERESA
DIAZ
TRUJILO
Septiem

Todos Santos, Guatemala, **1993**

Zunil, Guatemala, **1993**
Zunil, Guatemala, **1993**
Bogota, Colombia, **1991**

Patzcuaro, Mexico, **1992**

Patzcuaro, Mexico, **1992**

Todos Santos, Guatemala, **1993**

Zunil, Guatemala, **1993**

Salvador, Brazil, **1994**

Patzcuaro, Mexico, **1992**

Real De Cartorce, Mexico, **1992**

Todos Santos, Guatemala, **1993**

Chichicastenango, Guatemala, **1993**

Business with Death

Bogota, Colombia, **1991**

Santiago Atitlan, Guatemala, **1993**

Salvador, Brazil, **1994**

Bogota, Colombia, **1991**

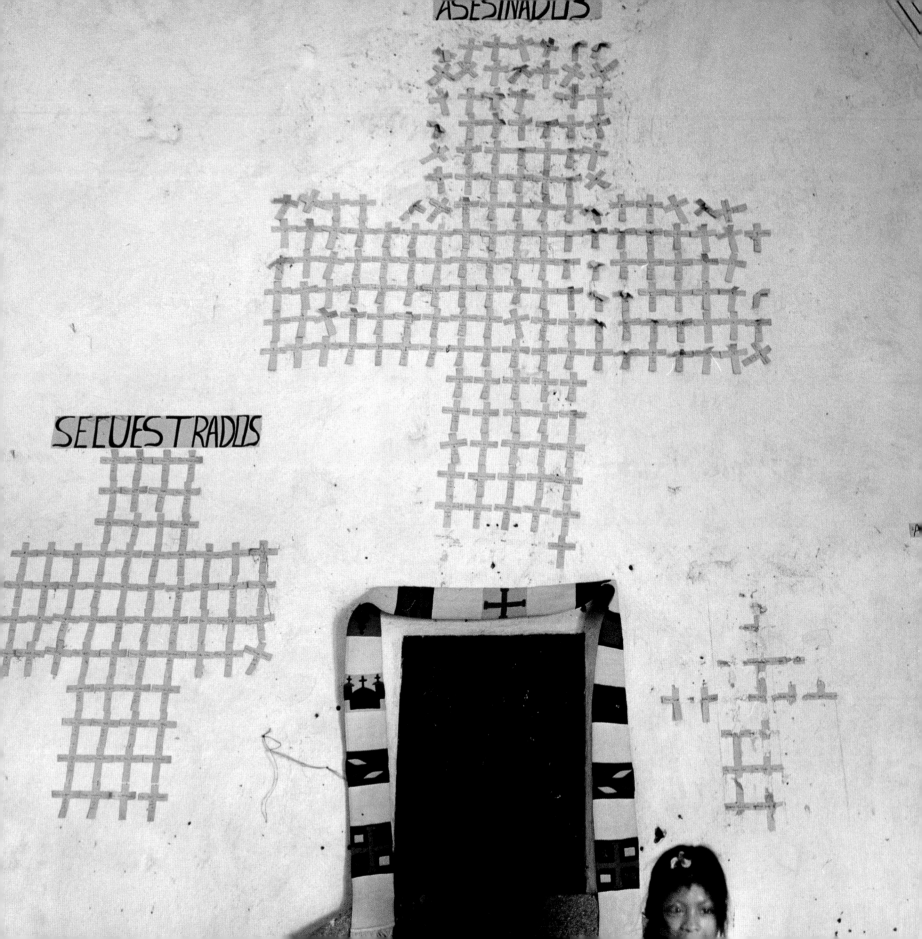

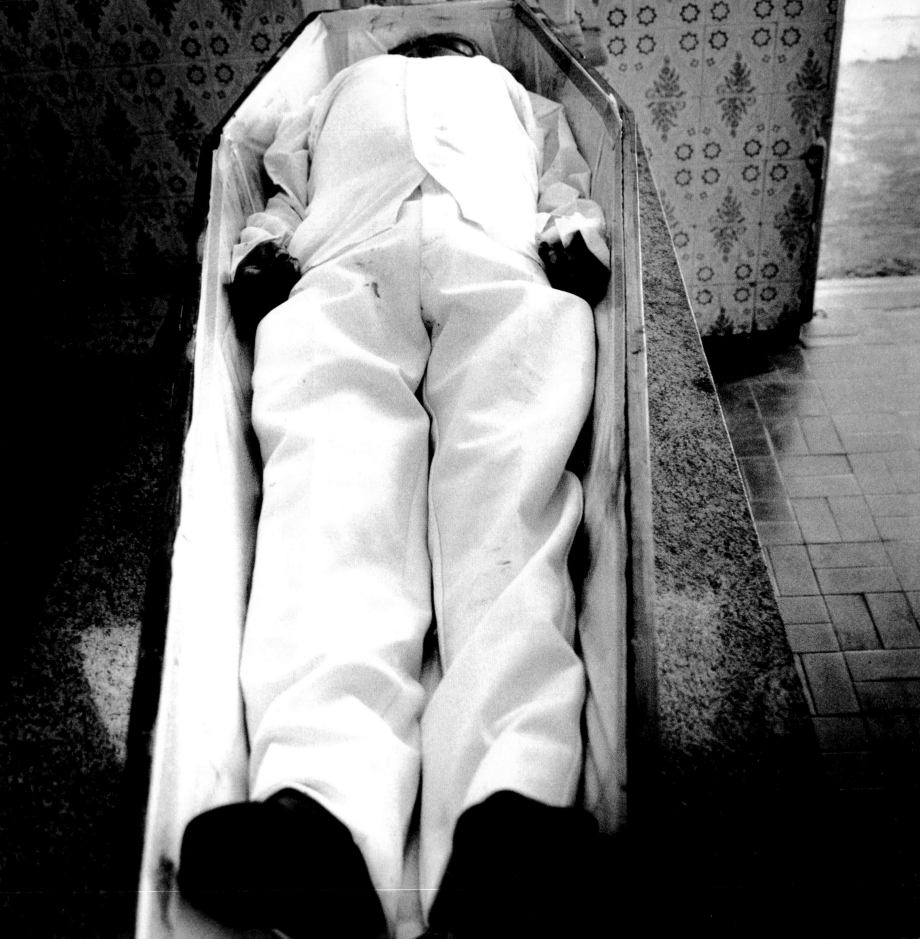

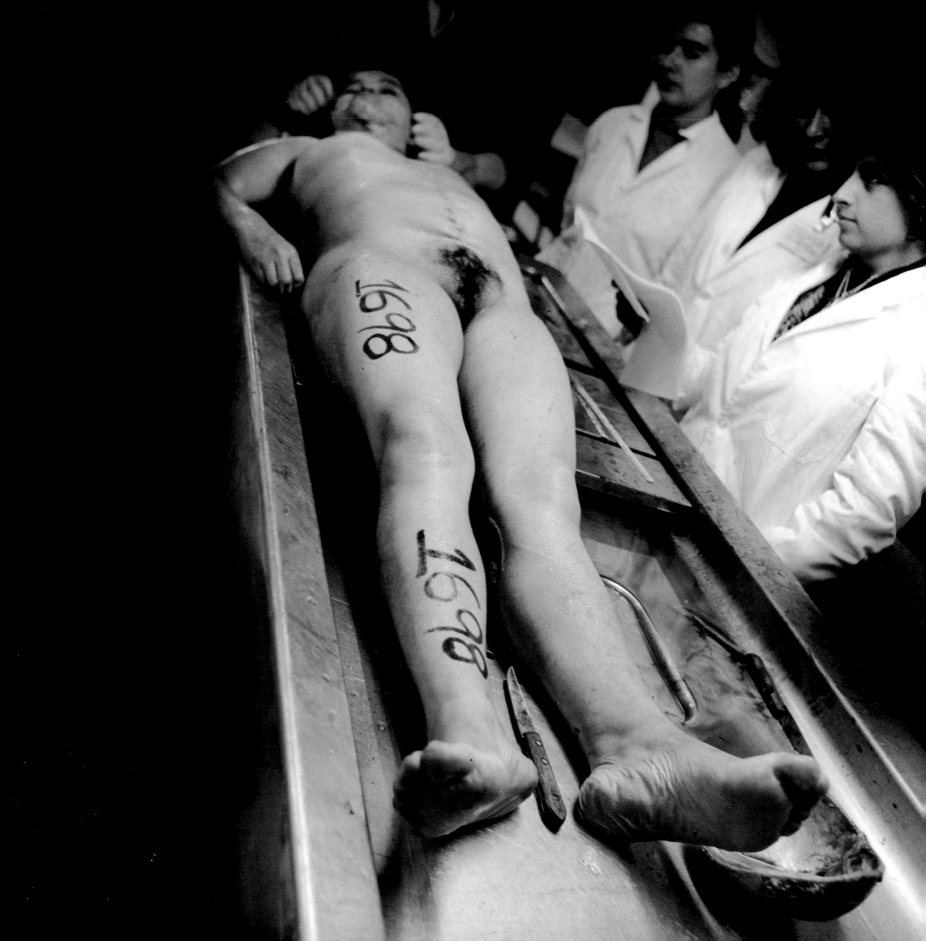

Bogota, Colombia, **1991**

Real de Cartorce, Mexico, **1992**

Concepcion, Guatemala, **1992**

Bogota, Colombia, **1991**

Bogota, Colombia, **1991**

Bogota, Colombia, **1991**

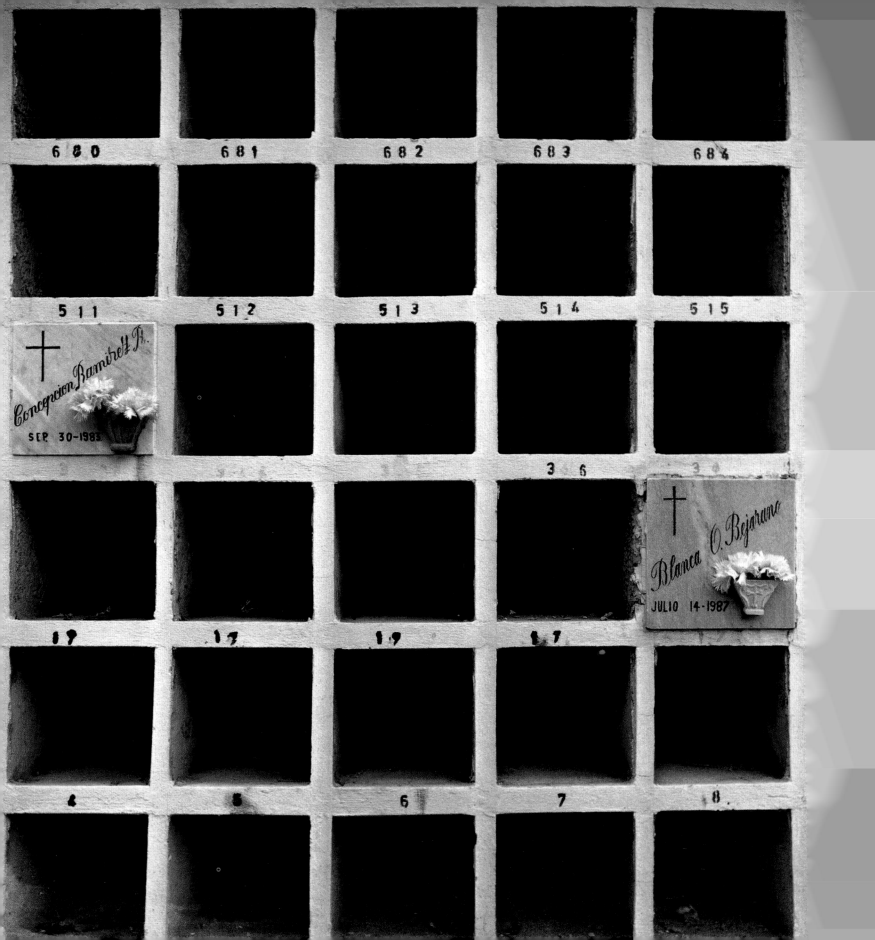

Havana, Cuba, **1994**

Bogota, Colombia, **1991**

Journal
Bastienne Schmidt

Lucy in the sky with diamonds. The Beatles accompany me to the airport. The Brooklyn-Queens Expressway runs through a forest of graves. The highway splits the cemetery into two sections – and in the background I see the Manhattan skyline. It is six o'clock in the morning, and the airport is virtually a ghost town. The flight to Bogota departs on time at 7:30.

Travel is my new home. On bus, on foot and in my mind I discover a world of images in which language is secondary. I just want to look, and not talk. That's how it was on our family trips. Through the endless expanses of Yugoslavia, our faces pressed to the windows of our old Ford Taunus. Figures approaching like shadows ... only to disappear behind us. It was like being in a cocoon; tensely awaiting each new sight, but securely protected against genuine encounters.

I'm still searching; searching for an understanding of my inner self through the outside world. Photography is my research tool and my solid rock, sometimes my excuse as well ...

The idea that I can hold on to moments and situations through photography is comforting. I want to preserve for myself everything that threatens to leave me.

My father is dead, and his death, which I would have been only too glad to flee, is my only guide through the Latin American landscape of grief, hope and mortality.

First Encounter with Death

Bogota, Colombia, April 1st, 1991

Monday is the day people go to the cemetery in Bogota. Black shadows move rapidly about, handling shovels and brooms like they do at home. For centuries women have been responsible for taking care of the dead here. They share the scissors used to cut up the bouquets. They hide the oil for the lamps behind a small door at the head of the grave. It is a precious commodity, not to be shared with anyone, since it is meant to provide the light that accompanies the dead throughout the night. But they share their pain by talking to each other about the dead. Death is a mark one bears in life. A young girl writes letters. She writes to a friend who was shot to death at the age of twenty. Every week she sticks a new message for him with wide tape on the grave plaque, only one of the many plaques embedded in a large wall – a wall of memory that keeps love alive.

The women appear to follow some secret choreography of gestures. They cross their arms firmly against their chest, fold their hands, close their eyes and turn their heads towards heaven.

Commerce flourishes all around them and their grief. Evangelists, dressed up fine in coats and ties, sell Bibles. A beggar – his abdomen covered with open sores – lies at the entrance to the cemetery. A priest unpacks his suitcase – stands there, holding his chalice, ready to say a blessing for money.

Bogota, Colombia, April 5th, 1991

A woman sits next to me at the cemetery. She is reading Espacio, a newspaper full of stories of love and bloody murder. Today's headline: Five People Killed. The photos show their bodies lying in the street, wrapped in white linen. I go to Calle 33A, the street where the funeral parlors are located. Three funerals are going on there at the same time – a simultaneity of death. Among the deceased is a woman who has died of leukemia. Sixty mourners have come. Many of them are young girls in school uniforms. Some of them cry; some just stare with expressionless eyes. I go unnoticed up to the third floor, moving from room to room ... white-clad children run about among the caskets. No one sits with the dead person in the next room. Loneliness even in death. A women enters the room. She asks if I am a relative – I nod my head.

Bogota, Colombia, April 16th, 1991

I visit the police headquarters, where I am introduced to Colonel Alvaro. He is friendly, shows an interest in my project and sees nothing strange about my quest in search of death. Death is a constant companion for him, too. In the courtyard I climb into a patrol car with four policemen. A police photographer accompanies the group. Night has come, and downtown Bogota is empty of people. Fires burn in the streets. The homeless cook their meals. Children lying in the entranceways of houses cover themselves with woolen blankets to keep warm.

It is a long night. Salsa and lots of espresso help combat fatigue. The police radio squawks in the background. The policemen have little to say.

It is Saturday night. On the weekends and paydays the death rate soars. Things are busiest between one and four in the morning. I find it hard to take photos. The events of a single night: a former police officer, a woman, has shot herself to death in front of her boyfriend. A pedestrian has been run over attempting to cross a highway; his body is mutilated beyond recognition. A man has been shot and killed in Bogota's red-light district. A one-year-old child has died of burns in the hospital.

Bogota, Colombia, April 17th, 1991

Today I have an appointment with Alberto, a journalist
with the newspaper La Prensa. But he doesn't show up.
His colleague Fernando takes me through the archives;
a mountain of photos documenting the violence of the
1980s, terrorist attacks and brutal government retalia-
tion. The photos show bombed-out buildings, burnt-out
cars, police at the scenes of bombing attacks. There are
pictures of weapons and sticks of dynamite; each object
bears a carefully written label ... containing an exact
description and designation of the photographed object.
Photography as surreal depiction of reality.
During these first few weeks I have seen so much of
death that an invisible film has spread itself over me and
keeps me from really feeling anything now. The reality
of violence has taken its effect.

Bogota, Colombia, April 19th, 1991

The paupers' cemeteries are located on the south side of
Bogota. It has just stopped raining. The ground is mud-
dy. The graves are modest in comparison to those in the
Cementerio Central. There are no marble statues, no
mausoleums for statesmen, writers and upper middle-
class citizens here. The endless walls bear only the
grave numbers and the names of the deceased.
A family of four stands in front of one such wall. The
grandmother's body is being exhumed. After three years
she is no longer entitled to a place of rest in the ground.
The rotting, worm-eaten casket lies in front of us. A
cemetery worker reaches into the coffin and pulls out
the bones. I recognize the remains of a lilac-colored
satin dress. There is a smell of decay and fresh earth.
Several women press their handkerchiefs to their faces.
A priest reads the mass. He blesses the box into which
the bones are laid. She is placed in a niche in the long
wall.

Through a leaning gate I enter a part of the cemetery or-
dinarily not accessible to the public. It is the last resting
place for the poorest of the poor.
Around the mass graves pillars of smoke rise from trench-
es in which clothing and refuse are being burnt. The
borders of the graves are lined with small, white crosses.
In the trench, naked corpses lie among pieces of old clothing and clumps of earth. Some of the bodies have been
hastily sewn together after autopsy. The curious on-
lookers are also the mourners at this funeral that is not a
funeral at all. Nevertheless, one after the other they toss
carnations into the grave of the unknown. Those unable
to afford a burial or who are unclaimed by relatives end
up here. Two boys sit on the edge of the ditch, sniffing
glue.
A black car arrives. It is known as *La Negretta*. A man in
blue workclothes gets out. His eyes are hidden behind
the thick lenses of his glasses. A cigarette dangles from
the corner of his mouth. He wears heavy plastic gloves.
From inside the car he and a helper pull out a stretcher
stacked with several corpses. There are men, women,
even an infant among the bodies. All of them bear numbers; all of them are swollen from the heat. There is a
smile on the man's lips. I'm told he is crazy. Three times
a week he makes the trip back and forth between the
Medicina Legal – the morgue – and the cemetery. I now
realize that the woman I heard playing the accordion a
few moments ago is blind. Here unseeing gaze seems to
fix on something above her, then wanders searchingly
over the cemetery. Our eyes do not meet.

Bogota, Colombia, April 21st, 1991

I have looked up a number of funeral parlors in the telephone book, and I call them. One of them is preparing a
body for burial this afternoon.
Juan, a man of few words, pulls the plump body from a
plastic bag and lifts it with a very few, precise move-

ments onto the table. In contrast to the face, the body seems to hold on to a vestige of life. The skin is white and taut – tender skin untouched by sunlight; it reminds me of my father's skin when we bathed him for the last time. I ask Juan if he likes working here, if the pay is good and why he has chosen this line of work. The work doesn't bother him, he says. It's just like any other ...

He earns sixty Dollars a month. Three other people work there. Together, they provide round-the-clock service. Juan makes a cut with a scalpel in the white flesh of the thigh – to me a sacrilege. A vein in the thigh is connected with a plastic tube to the jugular. Slowly, blood flows to the face; the frozen facial expression softens. Juan puts pants on the corpse and dresses the upper body in a striped shirt cut open in the back. Made up with rouge and lipstick, the body now looks like a corpse that wants to appear alive.

Medellin, Colombia, August 19th, 1991

I meet with Javier Tabon, a Catholic priest who lives and works in the *Barrio Nororientale* – a part of the city where drugs and violent death are everyday routine. The drug trade provides work. It has brought about the rise of a new profession, that of the *sicarios*, the professional killers. For the *sicarios*, killing is a job that puts food on their families' table. *Narcotráfico* has become an effectively organized big business.

Tabon talks about *sicarios* who confess their sins and go on with their lives as before. He speaks of a "schizophrenia of Catholicism." Mothers and the faith itself unknowingly provide support. Like the Mother of God, who forgives all sins, no mother asks a lot of questions when her son comes home with a VCR and a gold necklace. And when her son has been left to die in the street, his body riddled with bullet holes, she will light a candle for him every day and ask no further questions. Hundreds of the graves of victims of violent death occupy niches in a wall at the San Pedro cemetery. None of these men was older than twenty. Once again it is the mothers and girlfriends who make the daily pilgrimage to the cemetery. They write letters to the dead and attach them to the grave plaques.

"Querido Javier, ti quiero, por el primero cumpleaño sin ti" (Dear Javier, on the first birthday without you, I love you). A plastic heart and fresh flowers hang next to the letter.

Bogota, Colombia, August 20th, 1991

I have tried to get permission to visit the El Modelo prison; an ordeal of red tape. The elongated building is surrounded by a strip of barren ground and a barbed-wire fence three meters high. Women and children stand screaming at the top of their voices in front of the fence in hopes of getting their relatives to come to the barred windows. The inmates respond by hanging colored cloths in front of their cell windows.

I have been told there is one tract where all of the prisoners are *sicarios*. After lengthy negotiations I am finally allowed to enter the prison courtyard. A man leans against a statue of the Madonna, deeply engrossed in his newspaper. The sun is shining; the prison presents an idyllic appearance. The professional killers enjoy a number of privileges. They are allowed to take walks in an inner yard planted with geraniums and to play pool and soccer. They can quench their thirst at a juice bar. The barkeeper, a twentyeight-year-old wearing shorts and boasting a pot belly, is the star among them. He is said to have killed over thirty people. He tells me about his wife and his three children and about his job as a killer, which he plans to take up again once he leaves prison. Later he offers me some cocaine. There seems to be no shortage of that at the prison, either.

Gestures of Grief

Guajira, Colombia, August 26th, 1991

I travel through the Cienaga. The countryside is dried out. Huge trees lie on the parched ground, their roots pointing helplessly towards the sky. I arrive in Rioacha in the Province of Guajira sometime during the night. I meet Tonya, a woman from the Wayou tribe. She tells me about burials that take place in the desert near the border to Venezuela. I will have to wait four more weeks if I want to witness the event ...

In the company of Wilder, an economist, I travel to the most distant tip of the peninsula. We spend the night with Wilder's cousin Cecilia. She tells us stories ... stories like the one about the pregnant woman who once asked her advice regarding a health problem. At night, after the woman's visit, Cecilia dreamt that the woman's house was surrounded by spirits. The next morning she had three men dig up the ground. They found the skeletons of ten babies. As she explains to me, she had seen the dead spirits of the babies in her dream – for the dead, if not properly buried, cannot come to rest.

The return trip takes us through a river ford. The sun is low in the sky, and we want to get back before dark. We nearly reach the other side of the river before our vehicle gets stuck. The jeep turns slightly to the right, and within seconds the water rises so high that we have no choice but to escape through the windows. My camera bag is lost – I'm totally helpless without my camera ... We are stranded for two full days and spend the night with a fisherman's family. Late at night we sit in hammocks, roasting fish over a fire and gazing up at the crystal-clear starry sky. Wilder starts to talk. He knows a man in Bogota whose dog died. In order to transport the cadaver the man wrapped it in a package, which he had to leave standing for a moment while he made a telephone call. When he returned, the package was gone ...

The loss of my camera doesn't trouble me any more. It almost seems as if it had been just an excuse to find out something about other people's lives ...

Rioacha, Colombia, September 4th, 1991

Two days before I am to leave, Tonya calls to tell me that a burial is scheduled to take place in the Guajira desert. Every Wayou family has its own cemetery there. I go with Tonya to meet the family of the deceased. Three trucks carry the seventy members of the family – women, men and children – into the desert.

A Wayou funeral can go on for as long as two weeks. Grand funerals are prestigious events in the tribal community. Goats are slaughtered, people drink profusely and many families incur heavy debts in the process. We follow the barely passable roads to the cemetery. It is enclosed by chicken-wire. A few family graves cast in concrete can be seen. They are painted blue and white. In front of one grave I see baby-bottles, spoons, a bowl full of toys. It is important that the dead babies be able to play and eat; they should not be allowed to feel abandoned for a moment.

The casket bearing Juana, a young woman who has died in childbirth, lies under a straw canopy. The women touch it and take up a song of mourning that soon gives over to wailing and crying. Whenever it seems in danger of fading to an end, someone starts up again. The women remain with the dead throughout the day, while the men lie in their hammocks. The women wear veils and hold their heads in their hands. Nothing exists for them but their pain. I sit with them, crouched on the ground.

The men drink and become louder and louder until one of them approaches the women and collapses in tears in their midst. The goats are slaughtered in the late afternoon. Pieces of meat are hung on the fence. We all sit together in front of the fire and eat.

Puno, Peru, February 24th, 1992

I arrive on the night train from Cuzco. The train is a rolling market: peddlers selling glazed pig's heads, cobs of corn and *tamales* elbow their way through the gangway. They have to step over sleeping mothers and children. I had been warned about the skillfulness of Peruvian pickpockets. Arriving in Puno we move in a throng through a narrow gateway; there is a sudden jostling and confusion, I run in hopes of finding refuge in a hotel doorway. My camera bag has been sliced to pieces by razor blades.

I sit in the dark on the edge of my hotel-room bed. There is no electricity. I can hear the bellowing drunks from the street below. Carnaval has just begun in Puno. Someone tells me that there is a truck that travels from Juliaca to the Bolivian border. I want to take a trip around Lake Titicaca. From Puno to Bolivia and back. So I take my place with the other travelers on the bed of a truck. Seating on this journey is determined by the rule of the fittest. In this case, the women are the victors. Their territory is clearly marked off with sacks of Yucca, corn and potatoes. We arrive in Cumana, a small village near the Bolivian border. The next truck out doesn't leave until a week later. The local trader provides the only place for me to sleep. The night air is clear, but the temperature has dropped to below freezing. I lie on the bed, wrapped in a thin blanket, reading by candle-light. After two days, the room has become my home. I arrange every room I spend any amount of time in to suit me. It is my little ritual. I move the table and the chair to the window, from where I can best observe the goings on in the street. I lay my father's handkerchief on my pillow.

Cumana, Peru, February 25th, 1992

At night I dream: I am surrounded by people dressed up for a special occasion. Am I in a beauty contest? I'm de-clared the winner. They put a crown on my head and I walk to the podium. The gazes of the others bother me; I don't like being the center of attention. Only now do I realize that the judges are all dressed in black and I am wearing a death crown. Without knowing it, I have accepted death. From this moment on my fear of it is gone.

Cumana, Peru, March 1st, 1992

I've been in Cumana for five days.

I look out the window – a group of people is walking towards the church. What looks more like a parade is actually a funeral. Six men carry a coffin on their shoulders; they have come down from the mountains to bury their friend in the village cemetery. The women and children follow them at intervals in separate groups. The women carry bundles with personal possessions; the children bear home-made wreaths of flowers.

The cemetery seems abandoned. Man-high weeds and grass have overgrown the graves. The women sit down next to their bundles while the men look for a suitable place to begin digging a rectangular hole. When the coffin is lowered into the earth they lose control of their emotions. Since there is no priest in the village, one of the men, visibly moved, gives a speech in Quechua and Spanish. They are their own priests, their own grave-diggers.

A farewell with tears and home-made liquor. The mourners stand in a circle. On a cloth spread out on the ground each of them lays gifts in the form of coca leaves or cigarettes. One after the other they remove their hats, raise their glasses and drink to the deceased.

The women have prepared a funeral banquet outside the cemetery wall. They lay out yucca, beans and potatoes on cloths.

From here one has a view across the lake to the Island of the Moon, the birthplace of Manca Capac, the father of the Incas.

The Day of the Dead

Mexico City, Mexico, October 18th, 1992

My flight lands in Mexico City. Arriving in the chaos of this city of 25 million people is not a simple matter ... Theresa offers me a place to stay. She takes me to several different cemeteries. We talk about our father's deaths. Later on, we look at photographs of her family and mine. The photos she shows me are details of a world I do not know. What does she see? What do I see? We have different ideas. Each of us discovers her own history in the other's photos.

I love looking at photographs, studying each and every gesture, imagining that photography permits me to know someone without ever having seen him. Roland Barthes once said that although photography is not the representation of reality, it is evidence of what has been ...

Photography contradicts the impossibility of wanting to hold on to something and intensifies it at the same time. I remember a photo I had taken of my father and me at the hospital. We both smile for the camera. For my sake, he presented a second face – he never minded my photographing him. But what he was thinking each time I took his picture, he never told me. And the closer he came to death, the stronger was my compulsion to hold on to some part of him, secretly.

Memories to look at once again: the last Christmas together, the last family photo with the champagne glasses on the table. And then I took my father's picture after he died. I have since lost this photo.

A Look Back

The days before and after Christmas were ones of indescribable closeness. My mother, my sisters and brothers and I slept in my father's bedroom. We tried to get him to eat something. Ice-cream was the only thing he could swallow without pain. We bathed him.

We looked at old home movies: unsteady landscapes filmed by my mother from on board ship, sometimes a child making a face or running quickly away. My father at an archaeological site as he makes his way in the heat, his face red and his hair in a tangle, up towards the treasure house of Delphi.

I don't think he wanted to watch these movies. Did we want him to see his own life passing before him again – his life with us, as it was captured on film?

The transition from life to death was unnoticeable, insidious. My father stopped speaking. Only his eyes, so I thought, continued to question. When his breathing stopped, this breathing that we had watched over until the end, he was still with us. Our only comfort while we cried was the warmth of this body and his familiar smell. One after the other we broke down, but we supported each other. Afterwards, we washed him and dressed him in his brown corduroy suit. It was helpful to think that we were making such decisions as he would have wished. Where was the burgundy sweater he had worn to work nearly every day? The tie I had once brought him from Italy? We put his wallet containing a photo of us all and currency from many different countries in his jacket pocket and added the pipe tamper he had always carried with him. I cut off some of my hair and enclosed it my letter to him.

As long as we were busy, the pain was tolerable. The hard part was when the doctor arrived. Although we were all crying, we had to laugh as well, because the doctor looked like someone out of an Italian western. We wrapped my father's body in linen and carried him over the threshold to the hearse. We had a number of absurd things left to take care of. Choosing a casket, filling out forms, having obituaries printed.

At the funeral the pastor delivered an insipid sermon. I can't remember a single word of it; I only know that many people kept looking at us. I felt out of place.

Mozart's Requiem played from a tinny-sounding cassette player. We had argued about the music – the old against the young. Sophie and Benjamin were certain that my father would have wanted to hear Handle's Saul. Each of us was sure of being the one who knew him best. The funeral guests overran the house. A neighbor had baked a cake and their were hors d'oeuvres. I wore a blue blouse and a black skirt; my hair was combed back and tied with a ribbon. I had even put on lipstick. I was surprised at how I automatically concerned myself with such secondary things. What I really wanted was to retreat to my bed.

The Metaxa did its job ... we all got drunk. From the corner of my eye I observed my aunt flirting with a friend of my father's.

After it was all over the darkroom became the place I was most comfortable in. Outside of my family there was no one with whom I could have shared my pain. The darkness around me gave me comfort and protection from the world outside. In the weak light that gave everything a reddish tint I felt safe and secure. I looked for my family on old negatives, searching for situations and gestures that were familiar to me. Once in a while I would find a picture I had never seen before. At those particular moments it seemed like a miracle, a kind of proof that death was not final after all.

Mexico City, Mexico, October 27th, 1992

Ricardo introduces me to the director of the morgue in Mexico City. The official makes a very cultivated impression. He writes poetry in his free time. He is not the first person I have met on this journey who devotes himself to poetry after a day's work with death. He describes himself as the advocate of the dead. He tries to give those who can no longer speak a voice. Through the process of autopsy he forges a link to a past reality. He points to a drawer containing letters written by people who have committed suicide. They represent a kind of poetry for him. As he accompanies me on my way out – we pass through the conference room that is divided by two skeletons – he pulls a harmonica from his pocket and plays a song.

The students have arrived in the lecture hall. They gather around the corpse of a middle-aged man lying on a table in the middle of the room. Drops of blood fall into a plastic bucket. His body is untouched, but his head is mangled almost beyond recognition. A number hangs from his thigh. He is the 1,576th death this year. The students are supposed to learn how to use a scalpel. The atmosphere is friendly, actually quite cheerful. Two girls giggle and flirt with a male fellow student.

Patzcuaro, Mexico, October 30th, 1992

In Patzcuaro the morning is market time. It is a bedlam of traders and *campesinos* selling papier-mâché skeletons, sword lilies, gourds, bread-figures, candles, icons, sugar cane, spirits, chocolate death-heads and paper cut-outs of dancing skeletons.

The whole town has been in an uproar for days in preparation for the arrival of the dead. Like everywhere else in Mexico, people here believe that the dead return on the 1st and 2nd of November. On the *dias de los muertos*, the whole community celebrates, eats, laughs and cries together.

At the Patzcuaro cemetery a group of ten-year-olds pulls weeds. They repaint the fading inscriptions on the graves. The cemetery is their territory. They are not afraid of death, they say. Rusty coffins are stacked in one corner. There is a game going on: Who's afraid of the dead man? One after the other, the children run to the coffins and stick their hands into one of them. Then they run away, screaming.

A kindergarten teacher passes by with her class. Later on, I visit her at the kindergarten. The five-year-olds have been busy making death-head masks and painting them in bright colors for the past week.

That afternoon I take part in a procession. Nine young girls stand amidst garlands of corn and flowers on the beds of two trucks. They are dressed as angels. They wear long, white gowns and sewn-on wings made of cardboard and wire. A parade of people, led by a priest, follows the trucks. The Ave Maria can be heard. One angel falls to the ground and begins to cry.

The eve of the 1st of November is dedicated to the souls of children. When children die, the Mexicans say, one should not be sad; otherwise the *angelitos* will be displeased. In order to make the children happy, they place candy, bread, fruit and a cup of milk on the graves. The souls of children seeking the way back to earth can walk along paths laid out with leaves and flowers. The family of a deceased child spends the night at the cemetery, wrapped in heavy cloths, so that the little ones are not afraid. The candles burn until dawn. The following night is devoted to the souls of the adults ...

On the island of Lanitziou the houses are open to all visitors on this day. The decorated family altar is more than two meters high. It is made of shaped bamboo poles adorned with leaves and flowers. At its very top shines a crucifix. Bananas, pomegranates and pieces of copal are hung on lengths of wire. The faded color photo of a 60-year-old almost disappears among the surrounding pictures of saints and the many thick loaves of bread, the *pan de muertos*. At the highest point on the island, from which one can see out over the entire lake, there is a playing field. Three men stretch a huge fishing net between two basketball backboards. Then the women arrive to place bouquets of flowers in the net. These, too, are guideposts for the dead.

One family has come from the capital. Their daughter is buried here. The husband is a carpenter and was born nearby. "We must seek our final homes in the homelands of our ancestors," says the grandmother as she watches the dead girl's brothers placing Coca-Cola bottles and a basket of *tamales* at her grave. More and more people come as evening approaches. The street leading to the cemetery is one great sea of lights – candles and headlights in endless lines of cars. A procession passes by the graves in flickering candlelight.

The women awaken in the moist-cold dawn. They gather up their baskets. The flowers lie wilted and trampled on the ground. Everyday routine has returned.

Sacatepecez, Guatemala, October 31st, 1993

Arrival in Guatemala. Eleni picks me up at the airport. The villagers of Santiago Sacatepecez have spent the last ten days making colorful kites. Some are as large as five meters and covered with geometric patterns. On the Day of the Dead the villagers fly their kites. They are signs for the dead, meant to help them find their way to their graves. No sooner are the kites finally aloft than it begins to rain heavily. The kites, painstakingly put together with glue, are torn apart by the wind and rain in a matter of seconds. We look in vain for shelter among the graves.

Todos Santos, Guatemala, November 1st, 1993

The bus leaves at four in the morning. Our journey takes us from Huehuetenango through the highlands to Todos Santos. A flat tire forces us to walk the last few kilometers.

The first thing I do in Todos Santos is look for Miguel. I met him during my last visit here. Now in his early twenties, Miguel was an exchange student in a small town in Ohio. He speaks English and several Mayan dialects. He wants to become a doctor, spends the whole day in his father's pharmacy reading medical books. There aren't many like him in Todos Santos. Todos Santos means "all saints," like the upcoming feast day of the same name. Horse races are held each year in honor of the occasion. It is raining heavily. The first riders reach the village. One of them is so drunk that he cannot keep from falling off of his horse. Riders enjoy great prestige on this day. Most of the horses are rented. The races begin around noon. Miguel explains the origins of the race to me: During the period of the *conquista* the Indios were forbidden from riding horses on pain of death. The horse was a symbol of power for the Spaniards; to the Indios it symbolized their oppression. As a protest, the council of elders of the Indios ordered the horses taken into the highlands. They prayed to the gods for success and abstained from sex and alcohol in return. The plan worked. Since that time, horses are seen as embodiments of freedom.

At breakneck speed the horses race around a narrow, marked course. Winning is not important. The breathtaking speed is a reflection of the rider's fatalistic outlook. Fatal accidents are not uncommon. Drinking goes on all night and all through the following day. Then everyone makes the pilgrimage to the cemetery, where some devote themselves less to the memory of the dead than to feuding. Marimba sticks have disappeared. An argument breaks out. Two men wrestle noiselessly. The fight is no longer playful. It is a life and death matter. The crowd watches tensely as the drama unfolds; no one intervenes, until several hefty American tourists finally break up the fight. A little later I see the two combatants playing music together, as if nothing had happened.

Zunil, Guatemala, November 2nd, 1993

On the Day of the Dead Maxximon makes his rounds. He is revered as if he were a saint, although in other places he is referred to as Judas. Under the mistrustful eyes of the Catholic church the Indios of Zunil have preserved their own tradition. Carried on a chair at the end of a long procession, Maxximon is taken from his old hostel to a new one. His host family has already prepared a room for him. The saint wears a hat, sunglasses with reflecting lenses, a shirt and tie, a colored cloth and a poorly fitting suit made during the 1960s. The Indios believe that saints have the same needs and wants as people. Maxximon is fed three times a day and carried to his bed. Twice a day he is taken outside for a tour around the house to get some fresh air. The faithful touch him, full of awe and reverence, and ask him to ensure them a good harvest or health.

The burning cigar almost falls from his mouth as his chair is tipped to allow his bearers to pour alcohol into him.

The villagers of Zunil gather at the cemetery in the afternoon. It is located high on a hill, and its horizon disappears like the bow of a ship in the clouds. In the forest of corn stalks it is impossible to see a cross anywhere. The rhythms of marimba music are heard in the distance. The musicians proceed from grave to grave. A few women dance, fervently, with great abandon, and drunk. Two of them fall to the ground but manage to stand up again. One of the women's hair comes undone, and she begins to scream. While she screams, I sit on the ground, my arms and legs pressed close to my body, holding my camera in my hand.

List of Plates

Chronology

1961: born April 3 in Munich, Germany
1969-79: lives and attends school in Athens, Greece
1980: returns to Munich to study ethnology at the Ludwig Maximilian University; works in a psychiatric hospital
1983: moves to Perugia, Italy, to study painting and photography at the Accademia di Belle Arti, Pietro Vannucci
1987: receives Bachelor of Fine Arts Degree; moves to New York City and begins work at the International Center of Photography; works for the photographer Ralph Gibson.
1989-95: travels to Guatemala, Mexico, Colombia, Bolivia, Peru, Brazil and Cuba; starts work on the project Vivir la Muerte; regular contributor for magazines including *Frankfurter Allgemeine Magazin, Merian, New York Woman, Harper's Bazaar, Interview, Darkroom Photography, Vanity Fair*

Solo Exhibitions

1996 *Vivir la Muerte,* Houston Center of Photography, Houston, Texas; *Death Rituals,* Throckmorton, New York; *Vivre la mort,* Musée de la Photographie, Charleroi, Belgium
1995 *Fragments of Bogota; The New Documentarians,* International Center of Photography, New York
1993 *Vivir la Muerte,* Opsis-Foundation, New York
1992 *Storie di donne,* altered photographs, Galleria Planita, Rome; *Hunger, Art, Touch,* installations and photographs, Galería Libertadores, Lima, Peru; *Vivir la muerte,* Galería Kahlo-Coronel, Mexico City, Mexico
1991 *Memento mori,* photographs and objects, Alliance Française, Lima, Peru
1989 *Frammenti,* Galleria Atelier, Perugia, Italy

Group Exhibitions

1996 *Discoveries of Fotofest,* Houston, Texas; *Latin American Photography,* Brooklyn Museum, New York;

Deutscher Fotojournalismus, Deichtorhallen, Hamburg, Germany
1995 *On Death,* National Museum for Photography, Television and Broadcasting, Bradford, England; *Dia de los muertos,* Cable Access Gallery, Houston, Texas; *A Bestiarium,* Throckmorton, New York; *AFAP, Photography,* Prague, Czech Republic
1994 *The Photo-Essay,* Museum of Photography, Rotterdam, The Netherlands; *German Photo Prize,* Photokina, Cologne, Germany; *German Photo Prize,* Stuttgart, Germany; *AFAP,* Julia Cameron House, Island of Wight, England; *German Photojournalism,* Arles, France, *Dance of the Conquistadores,* Cavin Morris, New York
1993 *Compassion,* Hamilton Gallery, London; *World Press Photo,* Amsterdam, The Netherlands (Travelling exhibition)
1991 *The Interrupted Life,* The New Museum, New York; *Portraits,* Brand Name Damage, New York
1990 *Current Directions,* Museum of Contemporary Hispanic Art, New York
1988 *Animalia,* Arpino, Italy; *Expo Bari,* Bari, Italy
1986 *Opere recenti dell'Accademia Pietro Vannucci,* Academy of Fine Arts, Krakow, Poland
1985 *Colori nel mondo,* Rocca Paolina, Perugia, Italy

Awards

1993 Photoförderpreis, Landesgirokasse, Stuttgart, Germany
1992 2nd prize World Press Photo, Amsterdam, Netherlands
1987 Award of the Academy of Fine Arts, Bari, Italy

Collections

Museum of Modern Art, New York; Brooklyn Museum, New York; International Center of Photography, New York; The Museum of Fine Arts, Houston, Texas; Center for Creative Photography, Tucson, Arizona; Bibliothèque Nationale, Paris; Museet Fotografiska, Stockholm

Acknowledgment

My first and deepest gratitude is to the people in Guatemala, Mexico, Peru, Colombia, Brazil and Cuba, whom this book is about. In this unfamiliar world I have sought to rediscover parts of my own.
I thank my family, especially my mother Uta and my brothers and sisters Pascale, Florian, Benjamin and Sophie for their love, friendship and closeness, without which many things would have been impossible for me.
I thank Philippe for his love and understanding.
In Colombia, I would like to thank Tonya, Latoya and Colonel Alvaro.
My thanks to all of the people who accompanied me from the very beginning; espacially Ralph Gibson, Mary Ellen Mark and Miles Barth of the International Center of Photography. I thank Barry Taylor and Olympus for their interest in and support of this project. I am grateful to Barbara Millstein of the Brooklyn Museum for her open-hearted interest. My thanks to Charlie Stainback of the International Center of Photography for giving me the opportunity to show my work in a totally different setting. I also thank Robert Pledge for his support.
I thank the *FAZ-Magazin* and Thomas Schröder for making several of my trips to Latin America possible. I wish to thank Peter Hammel and Carolin Bohlmann for their friendship and their assistance with the manuscript.
Thanks to Edward J. Sullivan and Dr. Karl Steinorth for their introductory essays. Thanks as well to Mirjam Ghisleni-Stemmle for her insightful editing of my diary and to Dr. Thomas N. Stemmle for believing in the power of the pictures.
Special thanks are due to Hans-Georg Pospischil, who has stood behind this project from its inception, and without whose assistance and support it could never have been realized.

Thanks to the spirits and the gods who called me to life.

Copyright © 1996 by EDITION STEMMLE AG, 8802 Kilchberg/Zurich, Switzerland.

Reproduction copyright by
Bastienne Schmidt, New York
Text copyright by the authors
Translation from the German by John S. Southard
Editorial direction by Mirjam Ghisleni-Stemmle/
Nadjed el Khamash
Art direction and typography by
Hans-Georg Pospischil, Frankfurt (Main), Germany
Photolithography by Colorlito Rigogliosi S.r.l.,
Milan, Italy
Printed and bound by G. Canale & C. S.p.A.,
Arese, Italy

ISBN 3-905514-73-7